HOUGHTON MIFFLIN
HISTORY-
SOCIAL
SCIENCE

Contents

D1736474

Printed in the U.S.A

ISBN 13: 978-0-618-61851-4

56789-1413- 16 15 14 13 12 11 10

4500216391

UNIT 1 People and Places

UNIT 2 Places Near and Far

Practice Book

UNIT 3 Ways of Living

UNIT 4 People at Work

UNIT 5 America's Past

UNIT 6 America's Government

Name _____ Date _____

Skillbuilder: Parts of a Globe

Use the maps to follow the directions.

Northern Hemisphere

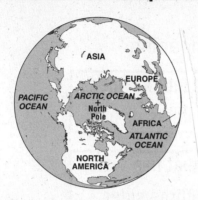

Southern Hemisphere

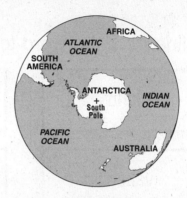

Western Hemisphere

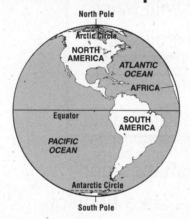

Eastern Hemisphere

Practice the Skill

1. Draw a line from the North Pole to the equator on one of the maps.

2. In which hemispheres is the South Pole found?

_____

3. If you went from North America to South America, you would cross a line called the _____.

Use with *Neighborhoods*, pp. 72–73

Vocabulary and Study Guide

landform   valley   island   peninsula   lake

1. Draw a line from the word to its meaning.

island		low land between mountains or hills
valley		land that has water on three sides
landform		land with water all around it
peninsula		the different shapes of the earth's land

2. The earth's water comes in many shapes and forms. One form is a lake. What makes a body of water a lake?

_____

_____

_____

_____

_____

Use with *Neighborhoods*, pp. 74–79

Skillbuilder: Use Intermediate Directions

Use the map to follow the directions and answer the questions.

Practice the Skill

1. Which city is southeast of Santa Fe, New Mexico?

_____

2. Draw a line between Selma, Alabama and Lincoln, Nebraska. In what direction would you travel to get to Lincoln from Selma?

_____

3. Which city is northeast of Columbus, Ohio?

_____

Use with *Neighborhoods*, pp. 82–83

Vocabulary and Study Guide

weather	climate

Use the words in the box to solve the clues and write the answer. Then find the words in the puzzle and circle them. Look from left to right, and from right to left.

1. The usual weather of a place over a long time

_____

2. What the air is like outside at any given time

_____

a	b	u	t	e	w	w	c	a
a	v	t	w	r	p	e	h	f
e	c	l	i	m	a	t	e	m
r	e	h	c	l	a	m	a	p
r	e	h	t	a	e	w	b	r
o	m	a	t	r	w	q	v	l

3. Tell one way the climate in your area affects the

way you live. _____

_____

_____

Vocabulary and Study Guide

region

1. A **region** is an area that has some features in common. Often the features are natural ones, such as landforms or climate. Draw a line from each feature to the correct kind of region.

Features   **Regions**

mountains		plant regions

deserts		climate regions

forests		landform regions

2. Human regions are areas where the people have features in common. Circle the letter of one example of a human region.

   A. grassy plains region

   B. language region

   C. desert region

3. Describe a landform region near your home or in your state.

   _____

   _____

   _____

Skillbuilder: Identify Main Idea and Details

Read the paragraph. What is the paragraph mostly about? What details tell more about this main idea?

  Almost one-third of Alaska is Arctic tundra. No trees grow in this region. The ground is frozen except in summer. In summer, low grasses and small flowers cover the tundra.

Practice the Skill

1. Write the main idea of the paragraph in the large circle.

2. Write one more detail in the small circle.

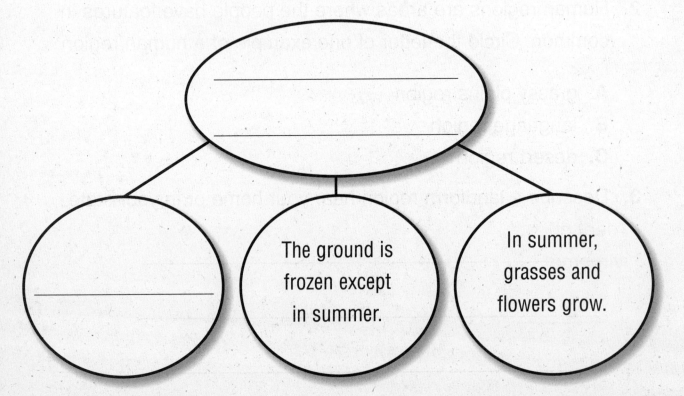

The ground is frozen except in summer.

In summer, grasses and flowers grow.

Vocabulary and Study Guide

| natural resource | environment |

Circle the words that correctly finish each sentence.

1. Something in nature that people use is a _____.

   natural resource   environment   consequence

2. The natural world around us is called the _____.

   synthetic   environment   resource

Some natural resources can be replaced and some cannot. Write them on the lines.

3. A natural resource that can be replaced:

   _____

4. A natural resource that CANNOT be replaced:

   _____

Tell one way that people change our natural environment. Write it on the lines. Draw a picture on a sheet of paper. Show how people can change the environment.

_____

_____

Vocabulary and Study Guide

custom	culture	immigrant	ancestor

Complete the word by reading the clue and choosing from the letters at right.

1. Something people usually do at a certain time

C U S T O M   O T E U C

2. The way of life of a group of people

C U L T U R E   L O C E R

Read the meaning and circle the correct word.

3. A person who moves from one country to another

ancestor   custom   immigrant   tradition

4. Someone in your family who lived before you were born

immigrant   ancestor   culture   values

5. What is one custom in your family? Tell why you like it. Write your answer on the lines. On a sheet of paper, draw a picture of that custom.

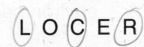

My Korean cloths that my dad wore when he was young.

Name _____ Date _____

Skillbuilder: Read a Timeline

Use the timeline to answer the questions.

Andrea's Family History

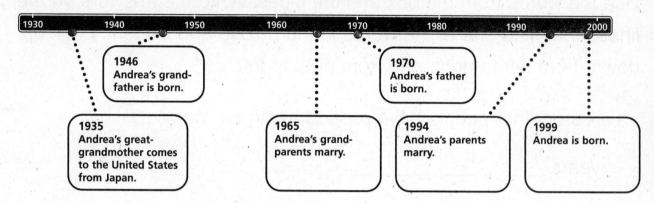

Practice the Skill

1. When did Andrea's grandparents marry? _1965_

2. Who was born in 1970? _Andrea's father_

3. What is the last event on the timeline?

Andrea is born

4. When did the last event take place? _1999_

Vocabulary and Study Guide

tradition	legend

Use the words from the box and the clues. Write the answers on the lines. Then find one of the words in the puzzle and circle it. Look up, down, from left to right, and from right to left.

1. A story that people have passed along for many

years ___legend___

2. Something that people do the same way year after

year ___tradition___

l	e	g	t	l	g	t
s	d	e	n	i	h	q
l	n	g	e	h	d	e
j	e	l	f	y	j	w
r	g	g	t	r	a	d
l	e	j	w	n	i	o
o	l	o	n	d	h	e

3. How is a legend different from any other story?
Write your answer on the lines.

___A legend is a story___

___that is passed from many years.___

Use with *Neighborhoods*, pp. 126–131

Skillbuilder: Conduct an Interview

Read the paragraph and follow the directions.

Practice the Skill

You plan to interview your neighbor, Mrs. Fuentes. She is now 82 years old. She came to the United States from Argentina as a young woman. Mrs. Fuentes plays the guitar and sings. She plays music from Argentina that she learned as a girl. What questions could you ask her about her life? Write three questions on the lines below.

1. _____

_____

_____

2. _____

_____

_____

3. _____

_____

_____

Use with *Neighborhoods*, pp. 134–135

Vocabulary and Study Guide

symbol   landmark   President
monument   memorial

1. Read page 140. Then use the words in the box to fill in the blanks.

Many buildings and statues honor America's

heroes. One is the Lincoln ___memorial___.

Another is the Washington ___monument___.

Each one honors an American ~~landmark~~ *President*.

2. Draw a line from the word to its meaning.

symbol	picture, place, or thing that stands for something
landmark	the leader of the United States of America
President	buildings or statues that honor heroes or events
monument	something like a sign or statue that helps people know a place

Vocabulary and Study Guide

national holiday	religious holiday

Circle the letter in front of the correct answer.

1. A holiday for everyone in the country is a _____.

   A. national holiday   **B.** religious holiday

2. A holiday for people who share a set of beliefs

   is a _____.

   A. national holiday   **B.** religious holiday

3. Ramadan is a _____.

   A. national holiday   **B.** religious holiday

4. Presidents' Day is a _____.

   A. national holiday   **B.** religious holiday

Name a holiday you like. Tell what kind of holiday it
is. Tell one reason you like it. On a sheet of paper, draw
a picture showing how you and your family celebrate
the holiday.

Christmas is my favorite holiday
because, I get presents.

Practice Book
21
Use with _Neighborhoods_, pp. 144–147

Skillbuilder: Make a Decision

Look at the picture of Carrie, her brother Tom, and her
friends.

Practice the Skill

1. What does Carrie have to decide?

Go play chess or ride her bike

2. Carrie made this chart about her decision. Use (+)
and (−) to mark <u>what is</u> good or not good about
each choice. Then circle the choice you would
make.

Play Game	Bike Ride
+ Checkers is my favorite.	+ Good exercise.
+ Tom will get to play.	+ Fun with friends.
− Only two can play.	− Tom will be sad.

Vocabulary and Study Guide

history

Circle the correct word to complete each sentence.

1. Everything we can know about the past is _____.

   A. pictures   **B.** present   **C.** history   **D.** stories

2. History is all that happened to people from far back
   in the past up to the _____.

   A. present   **B.** past   **C.** future   **D.** history

Circle the word that does NOT complete the sentence.

3. We can learn about history from_____.

   A. letters   **B.** stories   **C.** museums   **D.** babies

4. How do we know about the lives of American
   Indians of the past? Write your answer on the lines.

   _____

   _____

   _____

   _____

   _____

Vocabulary and Study Guide

explorer	journey

1. Find these words hidden in the box below. Find one word twice. Look up, down, and from left to right. Circle each word as you find it.

e	e	x	p	l	o	j	e
j	x	u	r	o	l	o	m
o	p	x	s	y	i	u	l
p	l	o	r	e	r	r	y
j	o	u	r	n	e	y	b
b	r	e	x	r	l	m	j
v	e	r	c	u	y	w	i
j	r	e	x	o	e	x	c
j	o	u	r	j	o	u	r

2. Look at the map of Marco Polo's journey on page 223. Then look at the map of Christopher Columbus's journey on page 224. What is one difference between the explorers' trips?

_____

_____

_____

Practice Book
34   Use with *Neighborhoods*, pp. 222–225

Vocabulary and Study Guide

| colony | settlement | colonist | Pilgrim |

Read the story. Fill in each blank in the story with a word from the box.

When we first came to Plymouth, it was a small _____. Today it is a large _____. There are more than 200 people and almost 40 houses. Now that I am eight, I am old enough to help Father in the fields. I bring in firewood, too, and tend the geese. My older sister helps Mother with the cooking and mending. In the evening, our parents teach us about _____ customs and traditions.

The life of a _____ is busy and sometimes hard. But I still have time for a game of marbles or leapfrog. If this year's harvest is good, each member of the _____ will join in a harvest celebration.

Skillbuilder: Identify Cause and Effect

Read the paragraph. Then answer the questions.

The Pilgrims did not have freedom to follow their religious beliefs in England. This problem caused them to come to America. Life was hard for the Pilgrims. Many were very sick during the first winter. They did not have enough food, so the Wampanoag helped them. The Wampanoag showed the Pilgrims how to hunt, fish, and plant. That helped the Pilgrims to stay alive.

Practice the Skill

1. What caused the Pilgrims to come to America?

_____

_____

2. What was the effect of the Wampanoag's help?

_____

_____

Practice Book

36

Use with *Neighborhoods*, pp. 238–239

Vocabulary and Study Guide

| independence |

Circle the correct word to finish each sentence.

1. _____ means being free from rule by another nation.

   A. Independence   **C.** Settlements

   B. Colonies   **D.** Revolution

2. Thomas Jefferson wrote the Declaration of _____.

   A. Revolution   **C.** Colonies

   B. Independence   **D.** King George

3. To gain independence, American colonists fought
   a _____.

   A. revolution   **C.** colony

   B. declaration   **D.** settlement

4. What was the Boston Tea Party?

   _____

   _____

   _____

Practice Book
37   Use with *Neighborhoods*, pp. 240–245

Skillbuilder: Compare Fact and Opinion

Read what the people say. Decide if they are telling facts or opinions.

It's not fair for the King of England to rule the colinies.

Thomas Jefferson wrote a Declaration of Independence.

Practice the Skill

Write the fact under **Fact.** Write the opinion under **Opinion.**

Fact	Opinion

Vocabulary and Study Guide

hero	invention

A hero may be a leader of people or the creator of an important invention.

Look at the two barrels below. Put the person named into the correct barrel.

Albert Einstein   Jackie Robinson   Sitting Bull
Golda Meir   Thomas Edison

LEADERS

_____

_____

_____

INVENTORS

_____

_____

_____

Vocabulary and Study Guide

transportation	technology

Complete the vocabulary word by reading the clue and choosing from the letters.

1. Using science to make things
   work better

   R H O Y G L K E

   T __ C __ N O __ O __ __

2. A way of moving people or things from
   one place to another

   H N T O R R O Y

   T __ A __ S P __ R __ A T I __ N

Circle the word that makes the sentence wrong.

3. Transportation is any way of moving _____.

   things   people   goods   thoughts

4. Technology has made transportation _____.

   faster   stronger   smaller   safer

Practice Book
40   Use with *Neighborhoods*, pp. 260–263

Skillbuilder: Understand Point of View

Read each point of view. Then answer the questions.

Juan

Kim

I think that baseball is the best sport. I can play it with my friends.

Gymnastics is the best sport. It makes me strong.

Practice the Skill

1. Why does Juan think baseball is the best sport?

_____

2. Why does Kim think gymnastics is the best sport?

_____

Name _____ Date _____

Vocabulary and Study Guide

communication

1. Draw a line from the sentence to the word that correctly finishes it.

Samuel Morse invented a	telephone.
Alexander Graham Bell invented the	Internet.
Benjamin Franklin got the mail carried by	stagecoaches.
Computers all over the world can communicate over the	telegraph system.

2. Look again at all the kinds of communication described in the lesson. List the ones you use.

_____

_____

_____

_____

_____

Name _____ Date _____

Vocabulary and Study Guide

1. We have three governments. Each one gives us different services. Put the following services into the correct barrel.

| Coast Guard | police | library | state roads |
| state parks | national parks | | |

Local Government
_____
_____

State Government
_____
_____

National Government
_____
_____

Write a word from the box to complete each sentence.

| government | capital | tax |

2. Governments collect money, called a

_____, to pay for services.

3. The city where people in state government work is

the _____.

Vocabulary and Study Guide

citizen	right	responsibility

Complete the vocabulary word by reading the clue and choosing from the letters at the right.

1. Something you may do

_ I _ H _   G C Y R W V X T

2. Something that you should do

R _ S _ O N S I _ I L _ T _   R E Z Y I B N P

3. A person who belongs to a place

_ I _ I _ E _   P C X Z N Y K T

Read the section "Citizens Have Rights" on page 293. Then choose the correct ending for the sentence below.

4. Rights can _____.

   A. make you angry   **B.** cost a lot   **C.** protect you

5. As a citizen of the United States, what is one right you have? Write it on the lines. _____

_____

_____

Vocabulary and Study Guide

law	judge

Circle the letter in front of the correct answer.

1. A _____ is a rule that everyone must follow.

   A. law   **C.** judge

   B. government   **D.** police

2. Police stop people who break the _____.

   F. government   **H.** rule

   G. law   **I.** judge

3. A _____ is someone who studies the law.

   A. citizen   **C.** judge

   B. police   **D.** government

4. Why do we have laws? Write your answers on the lines.

   _____

   _____

Name _____ Date _____

Skillbuilder: Read a Pictograph

Look at the pictograph. Use it to answer the questions.

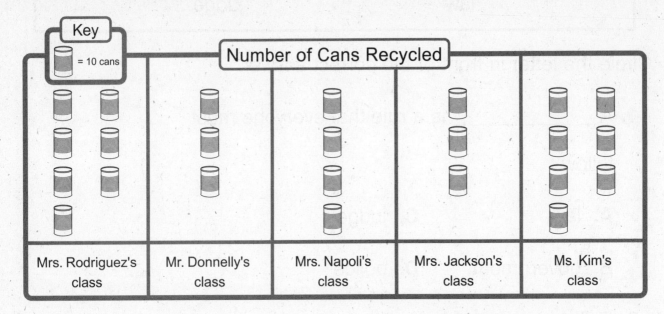

Practice the Skill

1. What does the pictograph show?

_____

2. Which classes collected the most cans?

_____

3. How many cans did each of these classes collect?

_____

Use with *Neighborhoods*, pp. 306–307

Vocabulary and Study Guide

1. Find these words hidden in the box below. Look up, down, from left to right, and from right to left. Circle each word as you find it.

vote	election	ballot

x	r	t	y	a	o	l	s	t	e
s	a	e	r	a	l	a	r	u	t
t	w	x	o	k	o	s	v	x	o
e	t	u	h	j	k	d	e	a	v
k	u	p	b	c	s	c	d	e	z
t	o	l	l	a	b	t	q	a	t
a	p	e	l	e	c	t	i	o	n

2. Write about what happens in an election.

_____

_____

_____

_____

_____

_____

Skillbuilder: Resolve a Conflict

Read the story. Then answer the questions.

Sam is seven years old. His twin sisters Jen and Ella are nine. Sam and his sisters disagree about where their family should spend the day. Sam wants to go to the zoo. His sisters want to go to the park for a picnic. How can Sam's mom and dad help resolve the conflict?

Practice the Skill

1. What is the conflict about?

_____

2. Here are some ways to resolve the conflict. Circle the letter that does NOT help resolve the conflict.

A. They go to the zoo today and the park tomorrow.

B. They go to the zoo and have a picnic lunch there.

C. The children stop talking to each other.

D. They go to the zoo in the morning and the park in the afternoon.

Vocabulary and Study Guide

Constitution	democracy	liberty	justice

1. Draw a line from the word to its meaning.

Constitution	fairness
democracy	freedom
justice	a plan for the government
liberty	government by people

2. Use the words from the box to fill in the blanks.

American leaders wrote our _____

more than 200 years ago. They did not want a king

to rule. They planned a _____, which is

government by people. In our Constitution, the

leaders wrote about _____, which means

"freedom." They also wrote about justice, which

means "_____."

Vocabulary and Study Guide

aid

Circle the correct word to complete each sentence.

1. When storms destroy crops in one nation, other

nations may send _____.

   A. postcards   **B.** animals   **C.** furniture   **D.** aid

2. Aid is _____.

   A. help   **B.** weather   **C.** trade   **D.** games

Circle the word that does NOT complete the sentence.

3. Aid can be _____.

   A. money   **B.** goods   **C.** flags   **D.** services

4. What kinds of aid might people need after a big
storm? Write your answer on the lines. Draw a
picture on a sheet of paper. Show one way citizens
can help people after a big storm.

_____

_____

_____

Practice Book
50   Use with *Neighborhoods*, pp. 322–325

Reading Skill and Strategy Practice

Reading Strategy: Summarize

Strategy Tips

- Think about the main ideas or the important parts of the text.

- Tell in your own words the most important things you have read.

1. **Pages 26–27:** Read this part of the lesson. Circle the best summary for this section.

   A. Children can play soccer on a team in their neighborhood.

   B. Leaders are people who guide others and make rules.

   C. Communities have helpers who do many kinds of jobs.

   D. A group is a number of people who live together or spend time together.

2. **Page 29:** Read this page of the lesson. Fill in the missing words from this summary.

   A _____ helps people know

   what they should and should not do. Most

   _____ have rules. Rules can

   help the group be _____.

Reading Skill: Compare and Contrast

This skill helps you see what is the same or different about two or more kinds of groups.

1. Read page 26. This part of the lesson tells about groups. Each part of the chart names one kind of group.

2. Name one more kind of group. Write it on the line.

3. Write the name of one person who belongs to each group.

Groups

family	school class	_____ _____
_____	_____	

Reading Skill: Main Idea and Details

The main idea is the most important thing about what you read. Details are other information that tell more about the main idea.

1. Read page 37. The main idea of this part of the lesson is written in the large circle. One detail is written at the end of each line.

2. Find another detail that tells about the main idea. Write it on the lines.

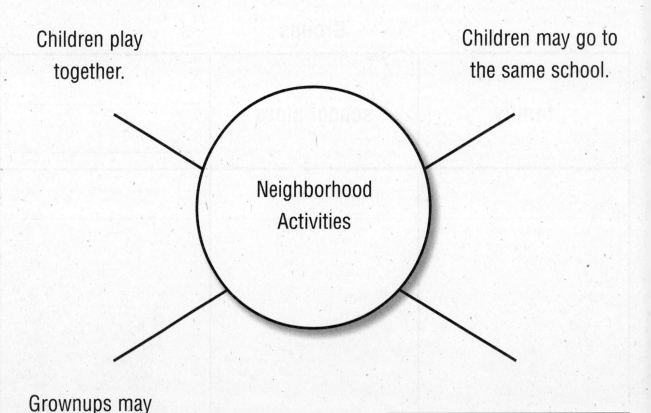

Children play together.

Children may go to the same school.

Neighborhood Activities

Grownups may work together.

_____

_____

Practice Book

5

SECTION **RS**

Reading Strategy: Predict and Infer

Here are some things to do before you read Lesson 3.
Doing these things will help you understand what
you read.

Strategy Tips

- Read the title and the headings. Look at the pictures. Think
  about what you have read so far.

- Tell what you think you will learn.

- Try to figure out things that the text does not say directly.

1. **Pages 46–47:** Read the headings. Circle the letter
   that tells what this part of the lesson will be about.

   Suburbs   Suburbs Depend on Cities

   A. Suburbs have many cars.

   B. Suburbs are filled with skyscrapers.

   C. Suburbs are communities near cities.

   D. Suburbs are communities in forests.

2. **Page 47:** Read this page. Why do people in
   suburbs depend on nearby cities?

   _____

   _____

Reading Skill: Cause and Effect

Often one event or action can cause something else to happen. A cause is why something happens. An effect is what happens.

1. Read page 44. This part of the lesson tells about cities. One event or action in a city can cause something else to happen.

2. Name what can happen in a city when many buildings are built close together. Write it in the other part of the chart.

Cause	Effect
Many buildings are built close together.	

Reading Skill: Compare and Contrast

This skill helps you see what is the same or different about farms and forests.

1. Read pages 53–54. This part of the lesson tells about rural areas. The chart shows how farms and forests are alike and different.

2. Fill in the chart to tell another way forests and farms are alike.

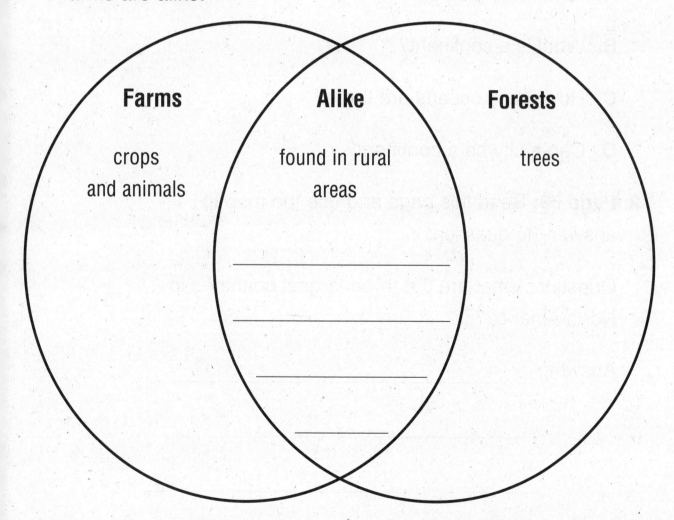

Farms

crops
and animals

Alike

found in rural

areas

_____

_____

_____

_____

Forests

trees

Reading Strategy: Question

Strategy Tips

• Ask questions that can be answered as you read.

• Ask questions that can be answered after you finish reading.

1. **Page 68:** Read the heading on this page. Circle the question below that you want to have answered as you read this part of the lesson.

   A. What is an address?

   B. What is a continent?

   C. How many oceans are there?

   D. Can a city be a continent?

2. **Page 68:** Read this page and use the map to answer the question.

   Question: What are the three largest countries in North America?

   Answer: _____

   _____

   _____

   _____

Reading Skill: Classify

This skill helps you understand and remember what you have read by organizing facts into groups, or categories.

1. Read pages 66–69. This part of the lesson tells about the address on an envelope.

2. Fill in the chart to show where you live.

Compare	Contrast
City	_____
State	_____
Country	_____
Continent	_____
	_____
	_____
	_____
	_____

Reading Skill: Compare and Contrast

This skill helps you see what is the same and different about the forms and shapes of land and water.

1. Read page 74–79. This lesson tells about the shapes and forms of land and water.

2. Name three more land forms and two more shapes or forms of water. Write them on the chart.

Land	Water
valley	ocean

Reading Skill: Main Idea and Details

The main idea is the most important thing about what you read.
Details are other information that tell more about the main idea.

1. Read page 84. The main idea of this part of the
   lesson is written in the large circle. One detail is
   written at the end of each line.

2. The main idea is about weather. Find one more
   detail that tells about the topic of weather. Write it
   on the line.

People want to know about weather.   Weather affects people's lives.

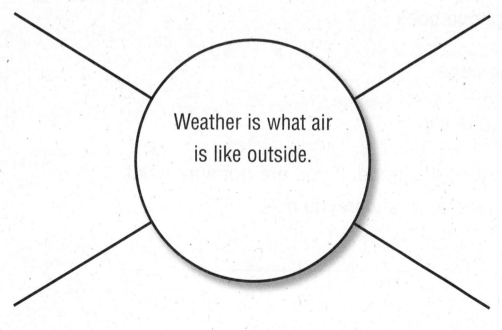

Weather is what air
is like outside.

Scientists measure weather.   _____.

Reading Strategy: Monitor/Clarify

Strategy Tips

• Ask yourself these questions. Do I understand this paragraph? What is the main idea?

• If you still do not understand something, reread it. Use the pictures and maps to help you. Read ahead.

1. **Page 92:** This page tells about regions. After you read the page, if you are still not sure what a region is, what can you do?

   A. reread the page

   B. use a phone book

   C. skip the page

   D. guess what it is

2. **Page 94:** Read this page. If you are not sure what plant regions are, what can you do?

_____

SECTION **RS**

Reading Skill: Main Idea and Details

The main idea of this lesson is about regions. The details are other information that tell more about regions.

1. Read pages 92–95. The main idea of this part of the lesson is written in the large oval. One detail is written in each of the small ovals.

2. The main idea states that a region is an area that has some shared natural or human feature. Find details that tell about kinds of plant regions. Write each detail on the lines.

Regions are areas with some shared feature.

landform regions

plant regions

1. _____

2. _____

Reading Skill: Sequence

This skill helps you understand the order in which
things happen.

1. Read pages 103–104. This part of the lesson tells
   about what happens when people cut down trees.

2. What happens first is shown in the first box. What
   happens next is shown in the next box. Find details
   that tell more about what happens. Write those
   details on the lines.

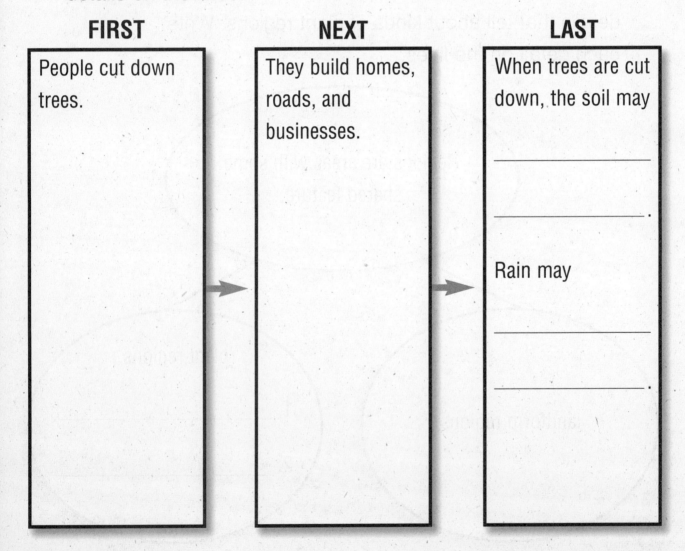

FIRST

People cut down trees.

NEXT

They build homes, roads, and businesses.

LAST

When trees are cut down, the soil may

_____

_____.

Rain may

_____

_____.

Reading Strategy: Summarize

Strategy Tips

- Think about the main ideas or the important parts of the text.

- Tell in your own words the most important things you have read.

1. **Page 117:** Read this part of the lesson. Circle the best summary for this section.

    A. It is fun to play games at a birthday party.

    B. People of all ages like to listen to music.

    C. Culture is the way of life of a group of people.

    D. People should speak more than one language.

2. **Page 118:** Read this page of the lesson. Fill in the missing words from this summary.

    People in the United States have many

different _____. Some cultures

come from _____.

Immigrants are people who move from one

_____ to another. Immigrants to this

country have brought their ways of living here.

Practice Book
31

Reading Skill: Draw Conclusions

Sometimes when you read, you have to figure out things that the writer does not tell you. This skill is called drawing conclusions.

1. Read pages 116–117. This part of the lesson tells about customs and cultures.

2. Read the facts in the small boxes. Then complete the sentence in the large box.

> Some families have piñatas at birthday parties.

> Some families eat pancakes at birthday parties.

> For birthdays, families have different
> _____.

Reading Skill: Main Idea and Details

The main idea is the most important thing about what you read. Details are other information that tell more about the main idea.

1. Read pages 128 and 129. The main idea of this part of the lesson is written in the large circle. One detail is written in one of the smaller circles.

2. Find another detail that supports the main idea. Write it in the other small circle.

People share their cultures in different ways.

1. Telling stories called legends

2. _____

Reading Strategy: Predict and Infer

Strategy Tips

- Read the title and the headings. Look at the pictures. Think about what you have read so far.

- Tell what you think you will learn.

- Try to figure out things that the text does not say directly.

1. **Pages 138–139:** Read the headings. Circle the letter that tells what this part of the lesson is about.

   A. America is a big country.

   B. America has many landmarks.

   C. America is south of Canada.

   D. America has many cities and states.

2. **Page 140:** Read this page. Why do you think people visit monuments or memorials? Write one reason on the lines.

   _____

   _____

   _____

Reading Skill: Classify

This skill helps you understand and remember what you have read by placing facts into groups, or categories.

1. Read pages 138–140. This part of the lesson tells about some different kinds of American symbols.

2. Look at the chart below. What headings would you put at the top of each group? Write the correct heading on each line.

_____	_____
Mount Rushmore Statue of Liberty	Washington Monument Lincoln Memorial

Reading Skill: Classify

This skill helps you understand and remember what you have read by organizing facts into groups, or categories.

1. Read pages 144–147. This part of the lesson tells about the holidays we celebrate.

2. Fill in the lines with the name of one more holiday in each category.

HOLIDAYS

National	State	Religious
Fourth of July	Maine and Massachusetts have Patriots' Day. California has _____ _____ _____	Ramadan

Reading Strategy: Question

Strategy Tips

- Ask questions that can be answered as you read.

- Ask questions that can be answered after you finish reading.

1. Page 160: Read the headings on this page. Circle the question below that you want to have answered as you read this part of the lesson.

A. How much do houses cost?

B. What is a continent?

C. What are needs and wants?

D. How do I know what I want?

2. Page 161: Read this page. Then write the answer to the question.

Question: Why do people have to make choices about what to buy?

Answer: _____

_____

_____

Reading Skill: Predict Outcomes

This skill shows you how to think about what might happen, based on what you have read.

1. Read page 161. This part of the lesson talks about how people make choices about what to buy.

2. Pretend you were given $10.00 for a birthday gift. You could buy a new book or a new board game.

3. Read the chart. Fill in the blanks. Tell what you would get with each choice. Then write your choice. Tell why you made that choice.

What I Give Up

1. If I buy a book, I give up playing the game with friends.
2. If I buy a game, I give up reading a new book.

What I Get

3. If I buy a book, I get _____ .

4. If I buy a game, I get _____ .

My Choice: _____

_____

SECTION **RS**

Reading Skill: Draw Conclusions

Sometimes when you read, you have to figure out things that the writer doesn't tell you. This skill is called drawing conclusions.

1. Read pages 166–168. This lesson tells ways to earn money.

2. Look at the facts in the two small boxes. Then write your conclusion in the large box. Tell why you think people work.

When people work, they earn money.	People always need to buy or use things.

People work so they can

_____

_____

_____ .

Reading Skill: Classify

This skill helps you understand and remember what you have read by organizing facts into groups.

1. Read pages 172–173. This lesson tells about goods and services.

2. Write the name of one more kind of goods and one more service on the lines in the chart.

Goods	Services
cars	doctors
apples	dogwalkers
_____	_____
_____	_____
_____	_____
_____	_____
_____	_____

Reading Strategy: Summarize

Strategy Tips

• Think about the main ideas or the important parts of the text.

• Tell in your own words the most important things you have read.

1. **Page 181:** Read this part of the lesson. Circle the best summary for this section.

   A. People should look at the prices of goods.

   B. It is important to get an education.

   C. Many people save their money in a bank.

   D. Some people like to go on long trips.

2. **Page 182:** Read this page of the lesson. Fill in the missing words from this summary.

   One service in a bank is called a

   _____. People put

   their _____ into a savings

   account. Each month, the bank adds a bit more

   money called _____.

   Interest helps the money in the account grow

   _____.

Reading Skill: Predict Outcomes

This skill allows you to think about what might happen, based on what you have read.

1. Turn to page 180. This part of the lesson tells about prices and choices.

2. Read the page and look carefully at the picture. Then fill in the blanks in the top box.

3. Fill in the blanks in the bottom box. Tell what you think Ken will do.

What I Learned

1. The amount of money you pay to buy something is the

_____.

2. Looking at prices helps people decide _____.

3. Ken has _____ to buy fruit.

What I Think Will Happen

4. Ken may buy the fruit that costs _____ or

the fruit that costs _____.

5. Ken does not have enough money to buy the fruit that

costs _____.

Reading Skill: Sequence

This skill helps you understand the order in which events happen.

1. Read pages 188–189. This part of the lesson tells how raisins get from the field to you.

2. What happens first is shown in the first box. What happens next is shown in the next box. Find three details that tell what happens last. Write them on the lines.

First	Next	Last
1. Workers care for the grapevines.	4. Workers take the raisins to factories.	6. Ships, trains, and trucks carry the packaged raisins.
2. They pick the grapes and place them in the sun to dry.	5. The raisins are checked, cleaned, and packaged.	7. The packages go across the _____ and around the _____ .
3. The grapes become raisins.		8. Stores _____ _____ .

Reading Skill: Cause and Effect

This skill helps you see the reason why an event or action can cause something else to happen. A cause is why something happens. An effect is what happens.

1. Read page 199. This part of the lesson tells how some farmers specialize, choosing to grow mainly one crop.

2. Look at the chart below. Then tell what can happen when farmers specialize. Write it on the lines.

Cause	Effect
1. Farmers in the United States specialize in growing wheat.	1. Farmers in the United States _____ _____ _____
2. Farmers in Costa Rica specialize in growing bananas.	2. Farmers in Costa Rica _____ _____ _____

SECTION RS

Reading Strategy: Predict/Infer

Here are some things to do before you read Lesson 1. Doing these things will help you understand what you read.

Strategy Tips

• Read the title and the headings. Look at the pictures.

• Tell what you think you will learn.

---

1. **Pages 213–215:** Read the headings. Circle the letter that tells what these pages will be about.

   The first people who lived in America

   A. lived in big cities.

   B. arrived here by boat.

   C. were American Indians.

   D. bought food in stores.

2. **Pages 216–217:** Read these pages. Why do people go to museums to see the items shown in the pictures? Write one reason.

   _____

   _____

   _____

   _____

Name _____ Date _____

Reading Skill: Classify

This skill helps you understand and remember what you have read by organizing facts into groups, or categories.

1. Read pages 214–215. This part of the lesson compares the way of life of four groups of American Indians. Fill in the lines with facts from the lesson.

Tribe	Homes	Clothes	Travel
Delaware	winter: longhouse summer: _____ _____	_____	by _____, on foot
Navajo	_____	animal skins, plants	on foot
Osage	winter: longhouse summer: small homes for travelers	_____	_____, by canoe
Shasta	winter: dwelling house summer: brush shelter	animal skins, _____	on foot, with _____ in winter, by canoe

Name _____ Date _____

Reading Skill: Compare and Contrast

This skill helps you see what is the same and different about two famous explorers.

1. Read pages 222–225. This lesson tells about Marco Polo and Christopher Columbus. The chart shows how they were alike and different.

2. Fill in the chart to tell details about the explorers.

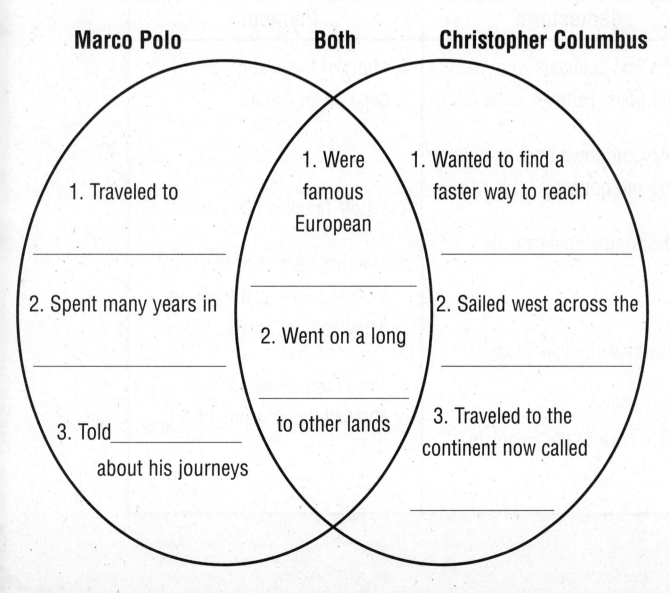

Marco Polo

1. Traveled to

_____

2. Spent many years in

_____

3. Told_____ about his journeys

Both

1. Were famous European

_____

2. Went on a long

_____

to other lands

Christopher Columbus

1. Wanted to find a faster way to reach

_____

2. Sailed west across the

_____

3. Traveled to the continent now called

_____

Reading Skill: Compare and Contrast

This skill helps you see what is the same and different about two North American colonies.

1. Read pages 230–233. This part of the lesson tells about two colonies, Jamestown and Plymouth. The chart shows how they were alike and different.

2. Fill in the chart to tell how the two colonies were the same and different.

Jamestown	Plymouth
1. The first colonists were men and boys. Families came later.	1. Many of the first colonists became known as _____ .
2. They cut down trees to build a fort and houses.	2. Whole families came together.
3. At first, the colonists ate _____ .	3. The first year, they faced sickness, fire, and freezing weather.
4. Nearby American Indians called the _____ gave corn to the colonists.	4. The Wampanoag Indians showed the Pilgrims how to _____ .

Reading Skill: Sequence

This skill helps you understand the order in which things happened.

1. Read pages 242–244. This part of the lesson tells how colonists in America got their independence from Great Britain.

2. Look at the timeline on the bottom of pages 242–243. Then find events from the lesson and the timeline that tell what happened. Write them on the lines below the correct dates.

• December, 1773

_____

_____

• April, 1775

_____

_____

_____

• July, 1776

_____

_____

_____

• 1783

_____

_____

Reading Strategy: Monitor/Clarify

Strategy Tips

• Ask yourself these questions. Do I understand this paragraph?
  What is the main idea?

• If you still do not understand something, reread it. Use the
  pictures and maps to help you. Read ahead. Sometimes an idea
  will be explained later.

As you read each part of Lesson 5, use these questions to check
your understanding.

1. **Page 252:** This page tells about heroes. After you
   read the page, if you are still not sure what a hero
   is, what can you do?

   A. look in a newspaper

   B. reread the page

   C. skip the page

   D. make up a meaning

2. **Page 256:** Read this sentence: Thomas Edison
   was a great inventor. If you are not sure what this
   means, what can you do?

   _____

Reading Skill: Classify

This skill helps you understand and remember what you
have read by organizing facts into groups, or categories.

1. Read pages 253–257. This part of the lesson tells
   about some American heroes of the past.

2. Look at the chart. One category names the heroes.
   The other category tells why they are important.
   Fill in details about these heroes. Tell the name of
   the hero or why that person is important. Write
   your answers on the lines.

American Heroes

Name	Why They Are Important
_____	helped the Lakota fight for their land.
Golda Meir	helped start the nation of Israel.
_____	became the first African American baseball player in the National League.
Thomas Edison	produced more than a thousand _____.
Albert Einstein	changed ideas in science about _____.

Name _____ Date _____

Reading Skill: Sequence

This skill helps you understand the order in which events happen.

1. Read pages 262–263. This part of the lesson tells how changes in transportation changed the community of Plainfield, Illinois.

2. Look at the timeline and the pictures on pages 262–263. Find details that tell when the changes in transportation took place. Write them on the lines next to the correct dates.

Transportation Changes Plainfield

- In 1834,

_____

_____

- By 1920,

_____

_____

- By 2004,

_____

_____

Reading Skill: Main Idea and Details

The main idea is the most important thing about what you read. Details are facts that tell more about the main idea.

1. Read pages 268–271. This part of the lesson tells how communication has changed over the years.

2. The main idea of this part of the lesson is written in the large circle. Some details are written in each of the smaller circles. Find more details and write them on the lines.

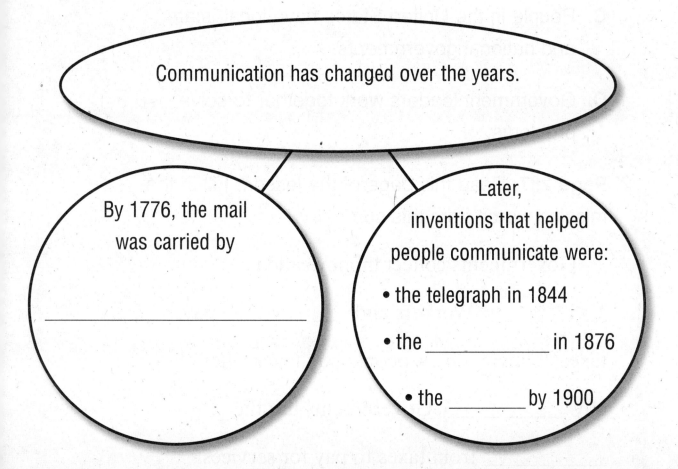

Communication has changed over the years.

By 1776, the mail was carried by

_____

Later, inventions that helped people communicate were:

• the telegraph in 1844

• the _____ in 1876

• the _____ by 1900

Practice Book
80

Reading Strategy: Summarize

Strategy Tips

- Think about the main ideas of the text.
- Tell in your own words the most important things you have read.

1. **Page 284:** Read this part of the lesson. Circle the best summary for this section.

   A. People in the United States speak many languages.

   B. Schools are special kinds of communities.

   C. People in the United States have local, state, and national governments.

   D. Government leaders work together to solve problems.

2. **Page 287:** Read this page of the lesson. Fill in the missing words from this summary.

   Governments collect money called

   _____. Workers and _____ pay

   taxes. In many states, people pay taxes when they

   buy _____. Governments use the

   _____ from taxes to pay for services.

Reading Skill: Draw Conclusions

Sometimes when you read, you have to figure out things that the writer does not tell you. This skill is called drawing conclusions.

1. Read pages 286–287. This part of the lesson tells about government services and the taxes that pay for them.

2. Read the facts in the first two boxes. Then draw a conclusion from what you read. Write your conclusion on the lines.

Governments give people services.	Governments collect money called taxes to pay for services.	What if workers and businesses do not pay taxes? Then people _____ _____ _____ _____

Reading Skill: Classify

This skill helps you understand and remember
what you have read by organizing facts into groups,
or categories.

1. Read pages 293–294. This part of the lesson tells
   about the rights and responsibilities of citizens.

2. One right and one responsibility are shown. Tell one
   more right and one more responsibility. Write them
   on the lines.

Rights	Responsibilities
speak freely	follow rules
_____	_____
_____	_____

SECTION RS

Reading Skill: Main Idea and Details

The main idea is the most important thing about what you read. Details are facts that tell more about the main idea.

1. Read pages 301–303. The main idea of this part of the lesson is written in the large circle.

2. Find three details that tell about the main idea. Write them on the lines.

Police tell people how to   Judges decide if someone

_____.   _____.

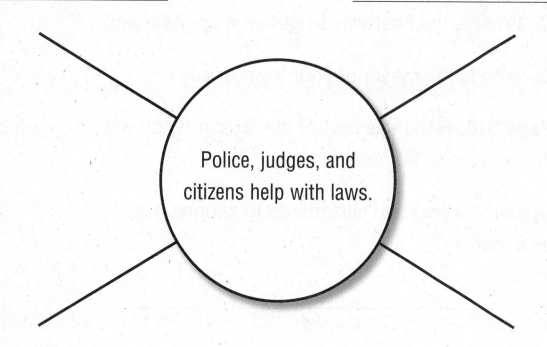

Police, judges, and citizens help with laws.

Citizens obey laws.   Citizens can work to

                                                        _____.

Reading Strategy: Question

Strategy Tips

- Ask questions that can be answered as you read.

- Ask questions that can be answered after you finish reading.

1. **Pages 308–309:** Read the headings on these pages. Look at the pictures. Which question do you want to have answered as you read this part of the lesson? Circle the question below.

   A. What are some rules in your classroom?

   B. How do people choose government leaders?

   C. What is the best way to get on a sports team?

   D. Who is the mayor of your town or city?

2. **Page 310:** Read this part of the lesson. Then write the answer to the question.

   Question: What can citizens do to choose the best leaders?

   _____

   _____

   _____

Practice Book
91

SECTION **RS**

Reading Skill: Sequence

This skill helps you understand the order in which things happen.

1. Read pages 310–311. This part of the lesson tells what people can do to choose the best leaders.

2. What happens first is shown in the first box. What happens next is shown in the next box. Find two details that tell what happens last. Write those details on the lines.

Before the Election

Citizens read newspapers, watch television, and ask questions about leaders.

During the Election

Citizens use ballots.
They mark their choices.

After the Election

Leaders need to _____.

Citizens need to _____.

Reading Skill: Classify

This skill helps you understand and remember what you have read by organizing facts into groups, or categories.

1. Read pages 318–319. This part of the lesson tells about the three parts, or branches, of our nation's government.

2. Look at the chart. It names the building where each branch of government works. It tells who works there and what their job is. Fill in the chart with details about each job.

Where	Who	Job
White House	President	_____
Capitol Building	Congress	_____
Supreme Court Building	Supreme Court Judges	_____

Reading Skill: Problem and Solution

This skill helps you think about a problem and how it could be solved.

1. Read page 322. This part of the lesson tells how nations help each other to try to solve problems.

2. Look at the chart. One part tells a problem a nation might have. The other part tells a possible solution. Complete the sentences to tell one possible solution for the problem.

Problem	Solution
Storms destroy crops in a nation.	Other nations may send _____. Aid can be _____ _____.

Section LS

Interactive Lesson Summaries

Summary: All Kinds of Groups

Groups

You are a part of many groups. Your family is a group. Your school class is a group. The actions of each person in a group make a difference to all.

Leaders

The leader of a band helps everyone in the band play music together. Teachers are leaders of their classes. In some classrooms, children take turns being leaders of activities or games. Most groups have leaders.

Rules

Most groups also have rules. Rules are meant to help people get along. They help people work or play together in the group. Following rules can help people in a group be safe. In some groups, people talk about their rules. They may make or change their rules together.

Before You Read

Find and underline each vocabulary word.

group *noun,* a number of people who work, live, or spend time together

leader *noun,* someone who leads others

rule *noun,* a statement that tells people what they may or may not do

After You Read

REVIEW **What groups do you belong to?** Circle two types of groups you belong to.

REVIEW **Why are rules important in a group?** Put a box around the paragraph that tells the answer.

Practice Book

1

SECTION **LS**

Summary: Living Together

Neighborhoods

You and your neighbors live in a neighborhood. Most neighborhoods have homes. Many neighborhoods also have stores, parks, and schools.

Neighborhood Activities

People in a neighborhood do many things together. The children may go to the same school. The grownups may work together to make their neighborhood look better or to make it safer.

Communities

Cities and towns are communities. A community may have many neighborhoods or just a few. Sacramento is a California city with many neighborhoods.

People in a Community

People in a community get together for many reasons. Perhaps the community has a fair every year. People from different neighborhoods may work together to get ready for the event. Others help out on the special day.

Before You Read

Find and underline each vocabulary word.

neighborhood *noun,* a part of a town or city
community *noun,* a place where a group of people live, work, and follow the same rules and laws

After You Read

REVIEW What activities take place in neighborhoods? Highlight two things people in a neighborhood might do.

REVIEW What are some reasons people get together in communities? Draw a box around the paragraph that tells the answer.

Summary: Cities and Suburbs

Cities

Many people live and work in cities. Cars, trucks, and buses crowd the streets. In some urban areas, tall buildings rise into the sky. Buildings are close together in cities, leaving little space for grassy yards. Children play in city parks.

Not all cities are alike. Not even all parts of one city are alike. One part of a city may have many office buildings close together. Another part may have a zoo, a river, a park, or smaller buildings that are farther apart.

Suburbs

Some people live in suburbs. Spring Valley is a large suburb of San Diego. In some ways, Spring Valley is like a city. With so many people, Spring Valley needs 18 schools. It has many grocery stores and other businesses.

Many people in suburbs depend on the nearby city for jobs, shopping, or fun. For example, people from suburbs all around San Diego can visit the famous San Diego Zoo.

Before You Read

Find and underline each vocabulary word.

urban area *noun,* a city or city land and its spaces

suburb *noun,* a community near a city

After You Read

REVIEW **What things can you see in urban areas?** Circle two things you might see in a city.

REVIEW **In what way do people in suburbs depend on cities?** Highlight three ways that people in suburbs depend on cities.

Summary: Rural Communities

Small Towns

Outside of cities and suburbs are rural areas. People in rural areas may live in small towns. Small towns have fewer stores, schools, and homes than cities or suburbs have.

Farms

Most farms are in rural areas. Farmers need a lot of space to raise animals or crops such as fruit and vegetables.

Forests

The wood people use for buildings, chairs, and other things comes from trees. Trees grow in forests. Forests are found in rural areas because trees need space to grow.

Markets

People in rural areas may send things they make or grow to markets in cities and suburbs. The wood, crops, and animals from rural areas are sold at the markets.

 Before You Read

Find and underline each vocabulary word.

rural area *noun*, a place with more open space than cities and suburbs

market *noun*, anywhere people buy and sell things

 After You Read

REVIEW **Why don't you usually find farms in cities?** Highlight the sentence that tells the answer.

REVIEW **Why are forests found in rural areas?** Underline the sentence that tells the answer.

Name _____ Date _____

Summary: Your Address

States in a Country

The letters U.S.A. stand for the country called the United States of America. California is a state in the United States. A state is part of a country. The United States is a country made up of 50 states.

Continents

If you were an astronaut looking at the earth from a space station, you would see mostly oceans. You would also see some very large bodies of land. Most of those large bodies of land are continents. The continents are North America, South America, Africa, Europe, Asia, Australia, and Antarctica.

The United States is on the continent of North America. The United States shares North America with two other large nations, Canada and Mexico. Canada is north of the United States, and Mexico is to the south. Seven small nations and many island countries are also part of North America.

 Before You Read

Find and underline each vocabulary word.

country *noun,* a land where people have the same laws and leaders

state *noun,* a part of a country

continent *noun,* a very large body of land

nation *noun,* another word for country

 After You Read

REVIEW How many states are in the United States? Circle the answer.

REVIEW What are two large nations that share North America with the United States? Highlight the names of those two countries.

SECTION **LS**

Name _____ Date _____

Summary: Land and Water

Landforms

Each of the many different shapes of the earth, such as a hill or valley, is a landform. A valley may have been carved out by a river running through it.

An island is land with water all around it. A peninsula is land that has water on three sides. Most of Florida is a peninsula.

A plain is flat or rolling land. Plains cover most of the middle of the United States. Other plains are along the Atlantic Ocean and the Gulf of Mexico.

Water

Water comes in many shapes and forms too. Most of the earth is covered with ocean water. Ocean water is salty.

A lake is a body of water with land all around it. Most lakes have fresh water. Lakes come in many sizes, from small mountain lakes to huge lakes such as Lake Superior.

A river is a long, moving body of fresh water. Rivers flow downhill into oceans, lakes, or other rivers.

Before You Read

Find and underline each vocabulary word.

landform *noun,* a natural shape of the land

valley *noun,* low land between mountains or hills

island *noun,* land with water all around it

peninsula *noun,* a piece of land that has water on three sides

lake *noun,* a body of water with land all around it

After You Read

REVIEW **How is a peninsula different from an island?** Highlight two sentences that tell the answer.

REVIEW **What is the difference between ocean water and the water in most lakes?** Underline the sentences that tell the answer.

Summary: Weather and Climate

Weather and Climate

People want to know about weather because it affects their lives. Scientists measure and predict the weather. Climate is the usual weather of a place. A climate can have different kinds of weather at different times of a year or even a day.

Living in Different Climates

Climates make a difference in the way people live. Palm Springs, California, has a climate that is hot and dry in daytime. People who live in Palm Springs need cool air in buildings year round. They need light clothes to wear.

Fargo, North Dakota, has a climate with very cold winters. People in Fargo need warm air in buildings in winter. They wear clothes that keep out snow and cold.

Farmers in some parts of California grow oranges. Orange trees do well in a warm climate. Some jobs fit one climate and not another. A snowplow driver, for example, would find work in places with cold snowy winters.

Before You Read

Find and underline each vocabulary word.

weather *noun,* what the air is like at any given time

climate *noun,* the usual weather of a place over a long time

After You Read

REVIEW **Why do people often want to know about the weather?** Underline a reason that people like to know the weather.

REVIEW **What is one way that climate makes a difference in what people do?** Circle the paragraph that tells how climate affects people in Palm Springs.

Practice Book

7

SECTION **LS**

Summary: Regions

Regions

A region is an area that has some shared feature. Natural regions are based on natural features such as climate or plants. Human regions are based on features such as the languages that people speak.

Landform Regions

Areas with shared landforms are landform regions. The United States has many landform regions. These regions include plains, highlands, and mountains.

Plant Regions

Places may be regions because they have the same kinds of plants growing naturally. The United States has large forest regions and grassland regions. It also has places where few kinds of plants grow. Some places are too dry for most plants. Other places are too cold and windy.

A plant region may be very different in different climates. Forests in Hawaii have trees that grow well in a hot climate. Trees in New England's forests need a cool climate.

Before You Read

Find and underline the vocabulary word.

region *noun,* an area that has some shared natural or human feature that sets it apart from areas around it

After You Read

REVIEW **What is a natural region?** Circle two things that can make up a natural region.

REVIEW **What are two kinds of plant regions?** Draw a box around the sentence that tells the answer.

Practice Book
8

Summary: Resources

Different Kinds of Resources

Air, soil, and water are natural resources. So are trees, rocks, oil. Some businesses depend on natural resources to make products. A rubber ball factory needs rubber. If the supply of rubber is low or runs out, the business might have to make a product that uses a different resource.

Some natural resources can be replaced. Others cannot. If you cut down a tree, you can plant another one. But if you keep pumping oil out of a well, someday it will run dry. You cannot get more oil from it.

Changing the Environment

Land, water, plants, animals, and people are all part of the environment. People change their environment. To build homes, roads, and businesses, people cut down trees. They drill wells for water and build dams across rivers.

In the past, people hurt the environment. Land and water got dirty. Some countries made laws to protect the environment and keep the air and water clean. Today, some parts of the world are cleaner.

 Before You Read

Find and underline each vocabulary word.

natural resource *noun,* something in nature that people use

environment *noun,* the natural world around us

 After You Read

REVIEW **What natural resources do you use?** Underline two natural resources that you use every day.

REVIEW **What natural resource cannot be replaced?** Highlight an example of a natural resource that cannot be replaced.

Name _____ Date _____

Summary: Families from Many Places

Family Customs and Cultures

Most families have customs. Mary's family sings in church on Sundays. Carla's grandma makes a piñata for Carla's birthday.

The clothes you wear and the foods you eat are part of your culture. Music and language are part of culture. Your religion and your customs are part of your culture too. You learn about your culture from your family, by doing things together and by talking together.

Many Cultures in One Country

The United States has many cultures. Some come from American Indian groups. Some come from the immigrant groups who have brought their ways of living with them.

Cultures from Ancestors

You can learn about your culture by learning about your ancestors. You can look at old pictures of them and things that belonged to them, such as letters or toys. Your name can tell about your ancestors too.

Before You Read

Find and underline each vocabulary word.

custom *noun,* something that people usually do at a certain time

culture *noun,* the way of life of a group of people

immigrant *noun,* a person who moves from one country to another

ancestor *noun,* someone in your family who lived before you were born

After You Read

REVIEW What is culture? Circle six things that are part of your culture.

REVIEW What are ways that children learn about their ancestors? Highlight ways you can learn about your ancestors.

Summary: Sharing Cultures

Traditions from Cultures

A tradition might be a special holiday meal or clothes for an event. Many families keep a tradition that comes from the culture of their ancestors. Families share their cultures by sharing their traditions with others.

Izumi's (ih ZOO mihz) grandmother learned origami, a paper-folding tradition, from her parents in Japan. She taught it to Izumi, and they taught it to Izumi's class.

Sharing Stories and Art

People share their cultures by sharing legends. Many legends come from a time when people told stories but did not write them. Later, people wrote them in books.

Art is another way of sharing cultures. People can see art in many different places.

Artists Who Teach

Some artists share their culture by teaching. Alan Hezekiah is a musician who teaches drumming. Alicia Adame-Molinar teaches Mexican dances.

Before You Read

Find and underline each vocabulary word.

tradition *noun,* an idea, a custom, or a belief that is kept or passed along in a family or other group
legend *noun,* a story that people have passed along for many years

After You Read

REVIEW **What is a tradition?** Highlight one example of a family tradition.

REVIEW **In what way can artists share their culture?** Underline the sentence that tells the answer.

Practice Book
11

SECTION **LS**

Name _____ Date _____

Summary: America's Symbols

Culture and Symbols

In the United States, people have traditions that have come from many cultures. They also share traditions that began here.

Symbols for the United States remind people that they are part of one country. The American flag is the symbol people use most often for the United States.

American Landmarks

A landmark is something that helps people know a place. A sign or statue may be a landmark. Many landmarks are symbols for America. Mount Rushmore is a landmark in the Black Hills of South Dakota. An artist and many helpers carved the faces of four Presidents in the stone of this mountain. This landmark reminds us of those leaders.

Monuments and Memorials

Many buildings and statues honor heroes or events. In Washington, D.C., the Lincoln Memorial, the Washington Monument, and the Thomas Jefferson Memorial help people remember three important Presidents.

 Before You Read

Find and underline each vocabulary word.

landmark *noun,* something that helps people remember a place

President *noun,* the leader of a country or nation

monument *noun,* something, such as a statue, that reminds people of heroes or events

memorial *noun,* something that reminds people of heroes or events

After You Read

REVIEW **Why are symbols of our country important to people?** Circle the sentence that tells the answer.

REVIEW **Why is Mount Rushmore an important landmark?** Highlight the sentence that tells the answer

Name _____ Date _____

Summary: We Celebrate Holidays

National Holidays

A national holiday honors someone or something that is important to the country. The date for a national holiday is the same everywhere in the country. Schools and many workplaces are closed so that families and friends can celebrate together.

State Holidays

A state holiday usually honors an event or a person who is important to that state. Schools and workplaces may be closed, but only in the state where people celebrate that holiday. In California, people celebrate Cesar Chavez Day of Service and Learning.

Religious Holidays

People who belong to a religion share a set of beliefs. They may have times each year to honor events that go with the beliefs of their religion. These times are called religious holidays. On religious holidays, people may eat special foods or go without food for a certain time. They may pray together, worship together, or have a meal together.

Before You Read

Find and underline each vocabulary word.

national holiday *noun,* a time when people honor events and people important to their nation

religious holiday *noun,* a time when people remember or celebrate a religious event

After You Read

REVIEW What is a way that state holidays are different from national holidays? Underline one way. They are different.

REVIEW What things do people do on religious holidays? Draw a box around the sentences that tell the answer.

Practice Book
13

SECTION **LS**

Summary: Needs, Wants, and Choices

Needs and Wants

Needs are things that people must have to live. Everyone has to have food, water, clothing, and shelter. Houses, trailer homes, and apartments are kinds of shelter.

Wants are things that people would like to have. People do not have to have those things to live. Everyone has wants and needs.

Making Choices

People cannot have everything they want. People have to make choices about what to buy. If they use all their money to buy one thing, they cannot buy something else.

Before You Read

Find and underline each vocabulary word.

needs *noun,* things that people must have to live

shelter *noun,* something that protects or covers

wants *noun,* things that people would like to have

After You Read

REVIEW Why do people have to make choices about what to buy? Highlight the sentence that tells the answer.

Summary: Work

Getting Things We Need

Hungry? Want an apple to eat? If you are the farmer who grows the apple, then you are a producer. If you are the person who buys the apple and eats it, you are a consumer. A consumer is someone who buys or uses things.

What if you grow the apple and eat the apple? Then you are a producer and a consumer.

Ways to Earn Money

When people work, they usually earn money. This money is their income.

One person's income may be earned from selling a painting he made. Another person may earn money by selling a crop she grew. Sometimes people sell their skills or their time. They are paid for teaching in a school or working in a shop. People do different kinds of work.

Before You Read

Find and underline each vocabulary word.

producer *noun,* a person who makes or grows something
consumer *noun,* a person who buys or uses goods or services
income *noun,* the money people earn

After You Read

REVIEW **What is a consumer?** Underline the sentence that tells the answer.

REVIEW **What work do people do to earn money?** Circle four types of work people do to earn money.

SECTION **LS**

Summary: Goods and Services

Goods

The things people make or grow are called goods. Goods are things that you can touch, such as cars, apples, and baseballs. Many goods are made in a factory. A factory is a building where people work to make goods.

Services

Some people are doctors, teachers, or dogwalkers. Those people do not make things. They provide services. Services are activities that people do to help other people.

 Before You Read

Find and underline each vocabulary word.

goods *noun,* the things that people make or grow to sell

factory *noun,* a building where people work to make goods

services *noun,* jobs people do that help other people

After You Read

REVIEW **What are some services you might use?** Circle three types of services people offer.

Summary: People Save Money

Prices and Choices

The amount of money you pay to buy something is the price. In stores, often the prices are printed on or near the things that people can buy. Looking at prices helps people decide what to buy.

Saving Money

Many people are careful not to spend all their income. Some save money so they can pay for what they want. They might save money in a piggy bank.

A Savings Account

Most people use a bank that has many services. One service is called a savings account. Instead of keeping their money at home, people put it in a savings account. They let the bank use the money. In return, the bank adds a bit more money each month. That money is called interest. Interest helps the amount of money in the account grow.

Find and underline each vocabulary word.

price *noun*, the amount of money consumers pay for goods and services

bank *noun*, a safe place where people can keep their money until they need to use it

savings account *noun*, a service provided by a bank to help people save money

After You Read

REVIEW **Why do people save money?** Highlight a reason people save.

REVIEW **What service at a bank helps people save?** Underline the sentence that tells the answer.

Summary: From Field to Market

From the Vine to You!

To make raisins, workers pick ripe grape bunches and put them on trays on the ground. As the grapes dry in the sun, they slowly become raisins.

Workers drive the raisins to the food processing plant to be checked, cleaned, and packaged. Ships, trains, and trucks carry the packages around the world.

Three Kinds of Resources

Raisin producers depend on natural resources. They need water, sunny days, and good soil. They also need human resources and capital resources. Human resources are people such as farm workers and machine operators. Capital resources are things such as tools, buildings, and trucks.

Scarcity

The earth has only so many human, natural, and capital resources. However, people have unlimited wants for goods and services. That is why there is scarcity. Because we cannot have all we want, we have to make choices about what to make or grow.

Before You Read

Find and underline each vocabulary word.

human resource *noun,* a person who helps make a product

capital resource *noun,* a resource such as a tool, building, or truck that is used to make a product

scarcity *noun,* not having enough resources to meet people's wants

After You Read

REVIEW **How do grapes become raisins?** Draw a box around the paragraph that tells the answer.

REVIEW **Why do people have to make choices?** Underline the reason we have to make choices.

Summary: People and Nations Trade

Barter

The exchange of goods or services without using money is barter. Long ago barter was the main way people got the things they wanted.

Trade

Many times, barter does not work very well. That is why most people today pay for goods and services in other ways, often with money. Whether people use barter or money, they are taking part in trade. You take part in trade when you buy an apple.

Depending on One Another

Farmers in the United States specialize in growing wheat, not bananas. Farmers in Costa Rica specialize in growing bananas, not wheat. When farmers specialize, that means they choose to grow mainly one crop.

Farmers in the United States sell their wheat to consumers in Costa Rica. Farmers in Costa Rica sell their bananas to consumers in the United States. People in countries around the world depend on trade to get the goods and services they want.

Before You Read

Find and underline each vocabulary word.

barter *noun,* the exchange of goods or services without the use of money

trade *noun,* the buying and selling of goods and services

specialize *verb,* to chose to do one thing very well or to produce one type of product

After You Read

REVIEW **How do you take part in trade?** Underline one way you take part in trade.

REVIEW **What does it mean to specialize?** Highlight the sentence that tells the answer.

SECTION *LS*

Summary: First Americans

History

You remember things that happened in the past. You also learn about the past from family stories. History is everything we can know about the past.

The First People in America

Our country's history starts with American Indians. Hundreds of American Indian groups already lived here more than 500 years ago. They depended on natural resources. American Indians used water, land, and plants in many different ways.

For example, the Shasta of northern California had different homes for winter and summer. They made clothing from animal skins and braided grass. For food, the Shasta gathered wild nuts and berries and other foods. They also caught fish.

American Indians used many natural resources to make and get the things they needed. To learn about the clothes, tools, and ways of living of American Indians in the past, you may visit museums.

Before You Read

Find and underline the vocabulary word.

history *noun,* the story of the past and of the people who came before us

After You Read

REVIEW **What is history?** Underline the sentence that answers the question.

REVIEW **Where might people today see things people made hundreds of years ago?** Circle one place people today might go to see things made long ago.

Summary: Explorers Travel the World

Explorers from Europe

Hundreds of years ago, European explorers traveled to other lands. They did not have cars or planes then. Their maps did not show much about the places they were going. Their journeys were filled with adventures.

Marco Polo

More than 700 years ago, an Italian named Marco Polo traveled to Asia. When he returned, he told thrilling stories about his journeys. Most Europeans knew nothing about Asia. Marco Polo's stories made people want to find out more.

Christopher Columbus

Christopher Columbus wanted to find a faster way to reach Asia. He read Marco Polo's stories and studied many maps. Then he sailed west across the Atlantic Ocean. His ships reached North America.

The journeys of Christopher Columbus changed what Europeans knew about the world. The new knowledge led to other changes for people of the Americas.

Before You Read

Find and underline each vocabulary word.

explorer *noun*, a person who travels to learn new things

journey *noun*, a trip; or *verb*, to travel

After You Read

 **REVIEW** **Why was Marco Polo important in history?** Highlight one reason Marco Polo was an important explorer.

REVIEW **Why did Christopher Columbus sail west?** Underline the sentence that tells the answer.

Practice Book
21

SECTION **LS**

Summary: Jamestown and Plymouth

American Land

After Columbus, more explorers traveled to North America, where they saw great natural resources in the land and water. American Indians already lived there. But European rulers sent people to settle there and take the land for their countries.

English Colonies

England was one country that started colonies in North America. The colonies began with small settlements. Two of them were Plymouth and Jamestown.

Jamestown and Plymouth

Life was hard for people in both settlements. Adults and children worked long hours. They faced sickness and hunger. Both settlements received help from and traded with nearby American Indians.

The first colonists in Jamestown were men and boys. Their families came later.

Many of the first colonists at Plymouth were Pilgrims. Many Pilgrims came to America with their families. They wanted freedom to follow their religious beliefs.

 Before You Read

Find and underline each vocabulary word.

colony *noun,* a place that is ruled by another country
settlement *noun,* a small community
colonist *noun,* a person who lives in a colony
Pilgrim *noun,* the name for the first colonists at Plymouth

After You Read

REVIEW **In what ways was daily life in Plymouth like daily life in Jamestown?** Circle the paragraph that tells the answer.

Summary: People from America's Past

Many Colonies

More people came from England to settle in North America. Some small communities grew into large towns and cities such as Boston and Philadelphia. People had to follow rules from the king of England, who was the ruler of Great Britain and its colonies.

The Declaration of Independence

More and more colonists wanted independence. Some began to act against British rules and taxes. King George, the British ruler, sent armies to control them.

Thomas Jefferson wrote words explaining why the colonies wanted independence. Those words became the Declaration of Independence.

The American Revolution

King George would not allow independence. He sent soldiers to fight a war against the colonists. The war lasted eight years. When it ended, the colonies had won independence. They became a new country called the United States of America.

 Before You Read

Find and underline each vocabulary word.

independence *noun,* being free from rule by another nation.

 After You Read

REVIEW **What did colonists do to show that they wanted independence?** Underline the name of the document Thomas Jefferson wrote to explain why the colonists wanted independence.

REVIEW **What happened after the American Revolution ended?** Highlight the two sentences that tell the answer.

Practice Book

23

SECTION **LS**

Summary: Past Heroes

Heroes

Some heroes are strong, brave leaders. Others are the first people to do something. Here are some heroes of the past who are still important today.

Sitting Bull was a leader of the Lakota nation. He was known for being powerful, brave, and wise. He always stood firmly for a way of life he felt was right.

Golda Meir helped to start a nation called Israel when she was a young woman. Later, as Israel's leader, she was one of the first women to lead a country.

Jackie Robinson was the first African American baseball player in the National League. People did hurtful things to him. But he did not quit. He set a great example.

Thomas Edison produced more than a thousand inventions. Some of them, such as the electric light bulb and sound recordings, changed people's daily lives.

Albert Einstein explained how light works. He changed our ideas about time and space. His work helped people understand the world.

 Before You Read

Find and underline each vocabulary word.

hero *noun,* a person who does something brave or works hard to help others

invention *noun,* something new that someone makes or thinks of

After You Read

REVIEW **What makes a hero?** Circle two qualities a hero might have.

REVIEW **Who was the first African American in the National League?** Highlight his name.

Summary: Communities Change

Transportation

When people travel or move goods, they use transportation. Inventors have used technology to make transportation faster, stronger, and safer. Technology has helped them make new kinds of transportation. New kinds of transportation have changed how people live in a community.

Transportation Changes Plainfield

In 1834, people came to Plainfield, Illinois, by stagecoach to settle the new town. Stagecoaches also brought travelers who stopped for food and rest.

By 1904, people rode streetcars on rails between towns. People came to Plainfield for vacations in a place called Electric Park.

About 1920, the first paved cross-country highway went through Plainfield. Cars and buses brought more people. Trucks brought goods quickly. More businesses opened.

Now many highways go around and through Plainfield. People have built more homes and schools. Families keep moving to Plainfield.

Before You Read

Find and underline each vocabulary word.

transportation *noun*, any way of moving things or people from one place to another

technology *noun*, the use of science to make things work better

After You Read

REVIEW What are three ways inventors have used technology to change transportation? Highlight the ways.

REVIEW What types of transportation have gone through Plainfield? Underline the different types of transportation.

Practice Book
25

 SECTION LS

Summary: Communication Changes

Communication in History

Communication is any way of sharing information. Communication has changed over the years.

In 1776, Benjamin Franklin got stagecoaches to carry mail between post offices. Letters reached people faster.

Samuel Morse invented a telegraph system in 1844. People could send coded messages and news quickly along wires.

In 1876, Alexander Graham Bell showed how telephones could send voice messages. With telephone wires strung across the country, people could talk even if they lived far apart.

By 1900, inventors had sent messages by airwaves. This led to the radio. In time, people had radios at home. Families could listen to music, news, or speeches. Later inventors found ways to make television work well.

By 1975, inventors had connected computers in networks. Soon computers around the world could join one huge network called the Internet.

Before You Read

Find and underline the vocabulary word.

communication *noun,* any way of sharing information

After You Read

REVIEW **How did the invention of telephones help people?** Underline the way that telephones helped people communicate.

REVIEW **How are computers around the world connected?** Highlight the sentence that tells the answer.

Summary: Government and People

Local Government

The government of a community is called a local government. People in your local government decide how to use money for schools, police, and other community needs. They try to solve community problems too.

Three Governments

Your state also has a government. Each state has a capital, which is the city where the people in a government work. The United States has a government, too. That is the national government. It is in Washington, D.C., the nation's capital. Everyone has three governments: local, state, and national.

Government Services and Taxes

Local, state, and national governments provide different services, such as parks, roads, and police. They collect money called taxes to pay for the services.

Before You Read

Find and underline each vocabulary word.

government *noun,* a group of people who work together to run a community, state, or country

capital *noun,* a city where the people in a state or national government work

tax *noun,* money charged by a government to pay for services

After You Read

REVIEW **What do people in local government do?** Highlight two things they do.

REVIEW **Why do governments need taxes?** Circle three things governments use tax money for.

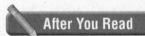

SECTION LS

Name _____ Date _____

Summary: Citizens Make a Difference

You Are a Citizen

You are a citizen of the community where you live and the nation where you were born. You can become a citizen of this country even if you were not born here.

Citizens Have Rights

As a citizen of the United States, you have rights that the government protects. You have a right to speak freely and to practice your religion. In the past, American Indians, African Americans, and women were not allowed to vote. They spoke out for their rights to vote and to be treated fairly.

Citizens Have Responsibilities

Along with rights, citizens have responsibilities. A responsibility may be following rules or doing a chore. It may be treating others fairly.

Being a Good Citizen

Good citizens care about people's rights. They try to make things fair and safe for everyone. Good citizens work together to solve problems.

Before You Read

Find and underline each vocabulary word.

citizen *noun,* a person who belongs to a place

right *noun,* something that a person is free to do, a freedom

responsibility *noun,* something that a person should do

After You Read

REVIEW **What rights do you have as a citizen?** Circle rights all United States citizens have.

REVIEW **How can you be a good citizen?** Draw a box around the paragraph that tells the answer.

Summary: Laws

Laws Are Important

Laws keep people safe and help them get along with one another. What do you think would happen if there were no traffic laws?

Police Help with Laws

Local, state, and national governments have laws. Police help with government laws. They tell people how to obey laws. They stop people who break laws.

Judges Help with Laws

A judge is someone who helps when people don't agree about laws. Judges know the laws well. They help decide if someone has broken a law. Judges say what people must do to make up for breaking laws.

Citizens Help with Laws

Citizens protect each other when they know and follow laws. When people obey a traffic law, they help keep others safe. When you follow laws in a park, you help others enjoy the park. Citizens help by choosing good people to make laws. Also, citizens can work together to make better laws.

Before You Read

Find and underline each vocabulary word.

law *noun,* a rule that everyone in a community, state, or country must follow

judge *noun,* a person who makes important decisions in a court of law

After You Read

REVIEW **What can citizens do to help with laws?** Circle the paragraph that tells how citizens can help with laws.

Summary: Leaders

Choosing Leaders

When you show or write a choice, you vote. Your school might have an election, which is a time when people vote. When you turn eighteen, you will have the right to vote in government elections.

Some government leaders make laws. Others, such as mayors, governors, and the President, make sure the laws work well. In elections, citizens choose leaders who they think can do these jobs the best.

Before You Vote

To choose the best leaders, citizens can read newspapers and watch television. They can ask questions of leaders.

Leaders and Citizens

In elections, citizens may vote on forms called ballots. Leaders who win elections need to keep listening to citizens. Citizens need to keep telling leaders what they want for their community, state, and country. Citizens and leaders together help governments work well.

Before You Read

Find and underline each vocabulary word.

vote *verb,* to make a choice
election *noun,* a time when people vote for their leaders
ballot *noun,* a form on which people mark their choices

After You Read

REVIEW Why should citizens vote in elections? Underline one reason that voting is important.

REVIEW What happens when citizens and leaders listen to and talk with one another? Highlight the sentence that tells the answer.

Name _____ Date _____

Summary: National Government

A Plan for Government

When the Revolutionary War ended, American leaders did not want a king to rule the new nation. The leaders met and wrote a new plan for the government. That plan is called the Constitution.

Important Words

The writers of the Constitution planned a democracy, which is government by the people. They used words that they believed were important in a democracy. One word was liberty, which means "freedom." Another was justice, which means "fairness."

Government in Three Parts

The Constitution is more than 200 years old. It describes a government in three parts, or branches. Each branch has its own building in Washington, D.C.

 Before You Read

Find and underline each vocabulary word.

Constitution *noun,* the plan of the government of the United States of America

democracy *noun,* government by the people

liberty *noun,* freedom

justice *noun,* fairness

 **After You Read**

REVIEW **What is the Constitution?** Highlight the sentence that tells the answer.

REVIEW **How many branches of government do we have?** Circle the answer.

SECTION *LS*

Summary: Our Nation and the World

Nations Help Each Other

The United States is one of more than two hundred nations in the world. Nations sometimes work out ways to help each other. If storms destroy crops in one nation, other nations may send aid. Aid can be money, goods, or services.

Leaders Work Together

Every nation has a government. Government leaders from different nations work together. They talk about how to make the earth cleaner and safer. Leaders have meetings about trade, health, and peace.

Meetings Around the World

World leaders meet together to discuss problems and try to find solutions. For example, the President of the United States met in Washington, D.C., with the President of Russia. The President of China met with the Prime Minister of Great Britain in Beijing, China.

Before You Read

Find and underline the vocabulary word.

aid *noun,* help

After You Read

REVIEW Why do leaders from different countries work together? Circle the sentences that tell what leaders talk about when they work or meet together.

REVIEW In which cities have some world leaders met? Highlight the cities that tell the answer.